5/67

CHEETAHS

by Jenny Markert

Content Adviser:
The Zoological Society
of San Diego

Published in the United States of America by The Child's World®
PO Box 326 • Chanhassen, MN 55317-0326
800-599-READ • www.childsworld.com

PHOTO CREDITS
© Andy Rouse/Getty Images: 16–17
© Anthony Bannister/ Gallo Images/Getty Images: 28
© Beverly Joubert/Getty Images: 6–7
© Chris Johns/Getty Images: 10–11
© Gallo Images/Corbis: 13
© Joseph Van Os/Getty Images: cover
© Manoj Shah/Getty Images: 23
© Mary Ann McDonald/Corbis: 19, 20–21
© Randy Wells/Corbis: 5
© Roger De La Harpe/Gallo Images/Corbis: 27
© Tim Davis/Corbis: 8
© Tom Brakefield/Corbis: 24–25
© Torleif Svensson/Corbis: 14–15

ACKNOWLEDGMENTS
The Child's World®: Mary Berendes, Publishing Director;
Katherine Stevenson, Editor

The Design Lab: Kathleen Petelinsek, Design and Page Production

LIBRARY OF CONGRESS CATALOGING-IN-PUBLICATION DATA
Markert, Jenny.
  Cheetahs / by Jenny Markert.
    p. cm. — (New naturebooks)
  Includes bibliographical references and index.
  ISBN 1-59296-632-2 (library bound : alk. paper)
  1. Cheetah—Juvenile literature. I. Title. II. Series.
  QL737.C23M268 2006
  599.75'9—dc22   2006001360

Table of Contents

On the cover: This cheetah is resting in the grass at sunset.

Meet the Cheetah!

There are only two species of cheetah: the African cheetah and the Asian cheetah.

Cheetahs were once common throughout large areas of Asia, Africa, and the Middle East. Now they are found mostly in parts of Africa.

The African plains are quiet in the late afternoon sun. A herd of gazelles moves slowly along, calmly munching on the grass. Little do the gazelles know that another animal is watching them! Crouched low in the nearby grass, a big cat moves slowly toward them. Once the cat is close enough, its streaks out of the grass. The startled gazelles scatter in every direction, trying to escape this fast animal. What is this speedy hunter? It's a cheetah!

This cheetah is running directly at the photographer. Does the picture make you feel as though you're moving?

What Are Cheetahs?

Cheetahs are the only big cat (lions and tigers are also big cats) that can purr.

Cheetahs often make chirping sounds, much like a bird.

Cheetahs are cats. They are also **mammals**, which means that they have hair and feed their babies milk from their bodies. Cheetahs are taller and slimmer than other big cats such as lions and tigers. Cheetahs can't roar like other big cats, but they can purr like a house cat. They can also yelp like a dog!

This cheetah is resting on a hill in Chobe National Park. The park is a protected area in the country of Botswana and covers 4,080 square miles (10,567 sq km).

Cheetahs weigh about 85 to 140 pounds (39 to 64 kg) and stand about 3 feet (1 m) tall at the shoulder. They have long, thin bodies and four long legs. They have arched backs and long tails, too. Their long tails help them keep their balance as they turn quickly while chasing other animals. The food animals they chase are called their **prey**.

The black stripes running from a cheetah's eyes down the sides of its face are important. They keep the sun out of the cheetah's eyes when it hunts on sunny days. Since these stripes are in the same place a teardrop would fall, they are called "tear stripes."

This cheetah has climbed a low tree branch to look for other animals in a nearby field.

How Fast Are Cheetahs?

A cheetah's nostrils, lungs, and heart are extra large to help them run at high speeds.

An average cheetah chase is about 3 miles (about 5 km) long, at about 45 mph (72 kph).

Cheetahs are the fastest animals on land. They can run up to 60 miles (97 km) per hour—as fast as a car on the freeway! Despite their speed, cheetahs don't always catch their prey. A cheetah can chase an animal for only a few minutes before getting tired. If the prey animal dodges and runs long enough, the cheetah gives up the chase.

10

This African cheetah is running at top speed in Chobe National Park.

What Are Cheetahs' Claws Like?

Cheetahs' paws also have thick pads on the bottom that help grip the ground during high-speed chases.

Cheetahs' claws are different from other cats' claws. Other cats can pull their claws back into their paws. This keeps the claws razor sharp, so the cats can climb trees and defend themselves. But cheetahs can't fully pull in their claws. Instead of being sharp and pointed, the cheetah's claws are dull.

Cheetahs can't climb tall trees or defend themselves as well as cats with sharp claws. But the cheetah's claws are very good for running! They stick into the ground like the spikes on a football player's shoes. Having such a good grip keeps the cheetah from slipping when it runs.

Even while this cheetah is at rest, its claws are sticking out. You can also see how thick and rounded the claws are; other cats' claws are much more pointed.

How Do Cheetahs Hunt?

Beginning about 5,000 years ago, people in Africa and Asia used cheetahs for hunting. Wild cheetahs were caught and trained, and used much like hunting dogs.

Cheetahs are **carnivores**, which means that they eat other animals. They find weak or sick animals the easiest to catch. Most wild cats hunt at night, but cheetahs hunt during the day. They usually hunt alone, but sometimes two cheetahs hunt together and share a meal.

This cheetah is watching wildebeests in the Masai Mara National Reserve in Kenya. Wildebeests are common prey for cheetahs, even though they are quite large. An adult wildebeest can weigh 600 pounds (272 kg)!

Cheetahs have excellent senses of eyesight, smell, and hearing, which help them find and hunt their prey. When a cheetah is hungry, it looks for a likely prey animal. Then it crouches low in the grass and waits. The spots on its fur help keep other animals from seeing it. This protective coloring is called **camouflage**.

The cheetah remains low in the grass. Slowly, it sneaks toward its unsuspecting prey. When it is close enough, the cheetah darts out and runs after the prey. Some prey animals are fast enough to get away. Others are no match for the cheetah's speed.

Cheetahs usually creep up on their prey until they are about 150 feet (46 m) away.

This cheetah is hunting in the Masai Mara National Reserve. This famous reserve is a protected area that covers about 124 square miles (321 sq km).

What Do Cheetahs Eat?

Cheetahs kill larger prey by clamping their mouth around the animal's windpipe. Without air, the prey dies in about five minutes. Smaller prey animals, such as rabbits, are killed with a quick bite to the head or neck.

On the plains of Africa, cheetahs find lots of different animals to eat. They prefer medium-sized animals such as antelope, impalas, and gazelles. They also eat smaller hares and ground birds. Sometimes, however, cheetahs hunt bigger animals such as zebras.

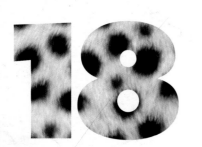

This cheetah caught a young antelope on the Masai Mara National Reserve. The antelope died a few minutes before this picture was taken, and the cheetah has not yet begun to eat its meal.

Usually, a cheetah eats its meal right where the animal falls. Cheetahs aren't strong enough to drag a large animal to a safer eating place. When a cheetah eats out in the open, other animals such as lions, leopards, and hyenas can see its fresh meal. The cheetah must gulp down its food before the other animals arrive. Often, other animals attack the cheetah to steal its food. If the cheetah doesn't eat quickly enough, it must leave hungry. Then it rests for a while and hunts again.

After eating their fill, cheetahs don't return to their kill. Cheetahs only eat fresh meat, and will leave the skin, bones, and organs of their kill for other animals to finish up.

Here you can see the same cheetah as it feeds on its meal. Cheetahs' faces and paws often get quite messy when they eat, so they spend a lot of time cleaning their fur after eating.

21

What Are Baby Cheetahs Like?

Cheetah cubs are born blind and without teeth.

A female cheetah usually gives birth to three to five babies, or **cubs**, at a time. This group of babies is called a **litter**. Cheetah cubs can be born anytime during the year. The mother gives birth in a safe place hidden from enemies. The young cheetahs have silver tufts of hair called a **mane** over their heads and backs. Scientists think the mane helps protect the cubs. From a distance, the cubs look like *ratels*—tough-skinned, smelly animals that aren't good to eat.

This young cheetah cub is resting in the shade on the Masai Mara National Reserve. You can see the lighter-colored mane standing up on the top of its head.

Very young cheetah cubs sleep a lot and drink only their mother's milk. As they grow bigger, they start walking and following their mother. They spend most of their time biting, pushing, and chasing each other. This play-fighting makes them strong and able to defend themselves.

The mother teaches the cubs how to hunt. First, she brings them a dead animal. The cubs watch her eat and copy her. Later, the mother cheetah knocks down an animal but doesn't kill it. She calls her cubs so they can learn how to kill it. Finally, the cubs must catch their own dinner.

This cheetah mother is showing one of her cubs how to hunt. She is letting the cub chase a baby Thompson's gazelle she caught.

Female cheetahs like to live alone, but males often travel together in small groups. Most groups of male cheetahs are made up of brothers.

Do Cheetahs Have Enemies?

Nine out of every ten cubs die before they are three months old.

If they safely make it to adulthood, most wild cheetahs only live to be about ten years old.

Lions, hyenas, and leopards sometimes kill cheetahs if given the chance. Eagles and other **predators** have also been known to carry off cheetah cubs that aren't with their mothers. But for the most part, cheetahs have few enemies in the wild. Instead, their biggest enemy is people. People are using more and more of the cheetahs' living space, or **habitat**, for farming and building. As a result, the number of cheetahs is dropping.

These young cheetahs live on the Phinda Resource Reserve in South Africa. This is a protected area that covers almost 66 square miles (171 sq km).

People also kill the animals cheetahs hunt for food. In some countries, laws have been set up to protect cheetahs. Many zoos have also started raising cheetahs in hopes of returning them to the wild. If we find ways to protect these fascinating animals, there will always be cheetahs racing across the African plains.

The name "cheetah" comes from a word meaning "spotted one" in India's Hindi language.

This cheetah mother is cleaning the face of one of her cubs in South Africa's Kruger National Park. This famous park is a huge protected area that covers 7,722 square miles (20,000 sq km).

Glossary

camouflage (KAM-oo-flazh) Camouflage is coloring that helps an animal hide or blend in with its surroundings. The cheetah's spots act as camouflage.

carnivores (KAR-nih-vorz) Carnivores are animals that eat only meat. Cheetahs are carnivores.

cubs (kubz) Baby cheetahs are called cubs. Cheetah cubs learn how to hunt from their mother.

habitat (HAB-ih-tat) An animal's habitat is the type of environment in which it lives. People have destroyed much of the cheetah's habitat.

litter (LIH-ter) A litter is a group of babies born to an animal at one time. A litter of cheetahs usually has about four babies.

mammals (MAM-mullz) Mammals are animals that have hair, are warm-blooded, and feed their babies milk from their bodies. Cheetahs are mammals, and so are people.

mane (MANE) A mane is an area of long hair around an animal's head. Baby cheetahs have a silver mane on their heads and backs.

predators (PRED-uh-turz) Predators are animals that hunt and eat other animals. Cheetahs are predators. Cheetah cubs are sometimes carried off by other predators.

prey (PRAY) Animals that are killed and eaten by other animals are called prey. Cheetahs catch their prey by running very fast.

species (SPEE-sheez) A species is a different type of an animal. There are only two species of cheetah.

To Find Out More

Watch It!

National Geographic Society. *Season of the Cheetah.* VHS.
Burbank, CA; Columbia TriStar Home Video. 1994.

Read It!

Becker, John, and Mark Clapsadle (illustrator). *Mugambi's Journey.*
Columbus, OH: Gingham Dog Press, 2005.

Hopcraft, Xan, and Carol Cawthra (illustrator). *How it Was
with Dooms: A True Story from Africa.* New York: Margaret K.
McElderry Books, 1997.

Hunter, Luke. *Cheetahs.* Stillwater, MN: Voyageur Press, 2000.

MacMillan, Dianne M. *Cheetahs.* Minneapolis: Carolrhoda Books,
1997.

Wood, Linda C., and Cynthia L. Jenson-Elliott. *Cheetahs
(Zoobooks series).* Mankato, MN: Creative Education, 1991.

On the Web

Visit our home page for lots of links about cheetahs:
http://www.childsworld.com/links

Note to Parents, Teachers, and Librarians: We routinely check our Web links to make
sure they're safe, active sites—so encourage your readers to check them out!

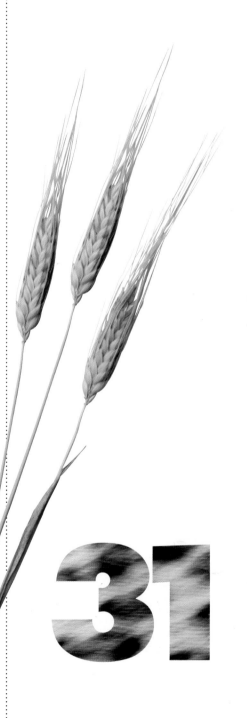

31

Index

About the Author

Jenny Markert lives in Minneapolis, Minnesota, with her husband Mark and children, Hailey and Henry. She is a freelance writer and high-school American literature teacher who loves traveling and adventure in all forms, whether it's sailing the lake on a windy day, hiking trails by moonlight, or helping her kids learn to boogie board when visiting the ocean. She is an animal lover and an environmentalist who believes, like the great American naturalist Henry David Thoreau, that "in wilderness is the preservation of the world." She is currently working on her second novel.